NEW BELIEVER'S SERIES

WATCHMAN NEE

READING
THE BIBLE

Living Stream Ministry
Anaheim, California

9

First Edition, November 1997.

ISBN 1-57593-965-7

Published by

Living Stream Ministry
2431 W. La Palma Ave., Anaheim, CA 92801 U.S.A.
P. O. Box 2121, Anaheim, CA 92814 U.S.A.

Printed in the United States of America

02   03   04   05   /   10   9   8   7   6   5   4   3

READING THE BIBLE

Scripture Reading: 2 Tim. 3:15-17; Psa. 119:9-11, 15, 105, 140, 148

I. THE IMPORTANCE OF READING THE BIBLE

Every Christian should read the Bible because it is "God-breathed and profitable for teaching, for conviction, for correction, for instruction in righteousness" (2 Tim. 3:16). It shows us many things that God has done for us and the way He has led men in the past. If we want to know the riches and vastness of God's provision for us, we must read the Bible. If we want to see God's step-by-step guidance for men, we must read the Bible as well.

God's speaking to man today is based upon what He has already spoken in the past. God rarely speaks things which He has not already spoken in the Bible. Even though a person may be quite advanced in his spiritual walk, God's revelation to him will still be confined to the words that He has spoken in the Bible. Hence, God's speaking today is merely a repetition of His own word. If a person does not know what God has spoken in the past, it is difficult for him to receive His revelation in the present because he lacks the basis for God's speaking.

Moreover, if God wants to speak something to others through us, He will also do it on the basis of what He has spoken in the past. If we do not know what God has said in the past, He cannot speak through us to others, and we are useless in the eyes of God.

This is why we need to let the word of God dwell in us richly. By letting His word dwell in us richly, we know His past ways and hear His present speaking. Only then can God use us to speak to others.

The Bible is a great book. It is a monumental work. Even if we spent our whole life on the Bible, we could only touch a part of its riches. It is impossible for a person to understand the Bible without spending time to study it. Every young Christian should do his best to labor on God's Word so that when he grows old, he can nourish himself and supply others with the riches of the Word.

Everyone who wants to know God must study His Word in a serious way, and every believer should realize the importance of reading God's Word from the very beginning of his Christian life.

II. BASIC PRINCIPLES IN READING THE BIBLE

There are four basic principles in reading the Bible: (1) Discover the facts, (2) memorize and recite the words, (3) analyze, categorize, and make comparisons, and (4) receive God's enlightening.

We must follow the sequence of these four steps when we read the Bible. We cannot jump from the third to the first step or from the first to the third step. First, discover the facts in the Bible. Second, memorize these facts. We must know and memorize God's Word accurately and exactly. We cannot afford to leave out or ignore any portion. If we do, our reading will profit little. Third, analyze, categorize, and make comparisons with the facts. After we have analyzed the facts accurately, categorized them properly, and compared them clearly before God, we will have the ground to take on the fourth point—God's enlightening.

The Bible contains many facts that are spiritual in nature. When a man's inner eyes are blind, he cannot see these facts. But once he discovers these biblical facts, half of the light contained in the Word will be his. God's enlightening is just His shining upon the facts that are recorded in His Word. Discovering the facts is half of our job in reading the Bible. When we read the Bible, the first thing we have to do is discover these facts.

For example, gravity is a fact. The law of gravity existed long before Newton, yet for thousands of years no one discovered it. One day, an apple fell on Newton while he was asleep under a tree. Through this he *discovered* the law of gravity. There is no question about the existence of facts. The question is whether or not these facts have been discovered.

For example, the Bible mentions something in some places and does not mention it in other places. One place mentions one thing while another place skips it. One place says it one way while another place says it a different way. The same word can be in the plural form in one place and in the singular form in another. Sometimes the Bible emphasizes the Lord's name while at other times it emphasizes a man's name. Chronology is clearly mentioned in some places, but totally skipped and seemingly neglected in other places. These are all facts.

A person who is good at reading the Bible is surely a careful person before God. He cannot be sloppy or muddled. Every iota or serif of the Bible is unalterable. God's Word says it, and it is so. The moment God's Word is opened up, you should know what its emphasis is. Many people are very careless. They listen to men's words carelessly and read God's Word carelessly. They do not see what God's Word emphasizes and are ignorant of the depths in His Word. The first thing a person has to do is discover the facts. Afterwards, he has to memorize these facts and analyze, categorize, and compare them. Only then will he receive light from the Lord. In this way he will get the supply and also supply others. He will receive nourishment and also nourish others.

Here I will give a simple illustration. If we read the Bible carefully, we will find the New Testament expressions *in the Lord, in Christ, in Christ Jesus,* etc. It never says *in Jesus* or *in Jesus Christ*. It only says *in Christ Jesus,* not *in Jesus Christ*. These are facts. We must memorize and jot down these facts one by one. Find where it says *in the Lord* and what the context is. Find where it says *in Christ* and what the context is. Find yet another place where it says *in Christ Jesus* and what the context is. If we know all these portions by heart, we can compare them. Why does it say *in Christ* in one instance instead of *in Jesus*? Why does one place say *in Christ Jesus* and not *in Jesus Christ*? Why does the Bible never say *in Jesus* or *in Jesus Christ*? What is the reason for this? When we analyze and compare the Scriptures in this way, looking to God for enlightenment, we will see something.

Once the light comes, everything will become very clear. *Jesus* is the name given to the Lord while He was on earth. *Christ* is the name given to Him after His resurrection when God anointed Him. "God has made Him both Lord and Christ." Do you remember these words in Acts 2? Christ is the name given to Him in His resurrection. In reading Romans we find the words *Christ Jesus,* which mean that the Christ today is the very Jesus who was on earth in the past. Christ Jesus is His name today. This means that the Christ today is the very Jesus who was on earth before. His name before resurrection was *Jesus Christ*. This name implies that Jesus would one day be the Christ. *Jesus* was His name when He lived on earth as a man. These two expressions—Christ being once Jesus, and Jesus eventually becoming Christ—mean two different things. Moreover, we can only be in *Christ,* not in *Jesus.* We can only be in *the Lord* and in *Christ Jesus,* not in *Jesus Christ.* When the Lord was on earth, we could not be in Him. If we had been in Him when He was on earth, we would have taken part in His cross and His redemption. This is contrary to the truth. We have no part in His incarnation at Bethlehem. He was the only begotten Son of God, and we have no part in that.

How then can we be in Christ? First Corinthians 1:30 says, "But of Him [God] you are in Christ Jesus." It does not say *in Jesus.* After the Lord Jesus died and resurrected, we became joined to Him in His resurrection. Through His death and resurrection, God has made Him the Christ, and God has joined us to Him through the Spirit. We received His life at the time of His resurrection. Regeneration does not come through incarnation but through resurrection. Now we should be clear.

This is the way to read the Bible. This is how we study the Bible. First, discover the facts. Then memorize, analyze, categorize, and compare these facts. After this pray to the

Lord and wait on Him; He will enlighten you and give you sight. These are the four principles of reading the Bible. We cannot skip any one of them.

Let us give another illustration. Consider the word about the coming of the Holy Spirit in John 14 and 15. In reading these passages, we must pay attention to the promise of the Lord Jesus and discover whether there are any special facts related to it.

John 14:16-20 says, "And I will ask the Father, and He will give you another Comforter, that He may be with you forever, even the Spirit of reality, whom the world cannot receive, because it does not behold Him or know Him; but you know Him, because He abides with you and shall be in you. I will not leave you as orphans; I am coming to you. Yet a little while and the world beholds Me no longer, but you behold Me; because I live, you also shall live. In that day you will know that I am in My Father, and you in Me, and I in you." What facts can we discover here? These sentences first use *He* or *Him* but later change to *I*. There is a change in pronoun. Here is a fact: The words *He* and *Him* have been changed to *I*.

According to the four principles of reading the Bible, how should we deal with this passage? First, we should discover the facts. In this case, the pronoun change from *He* to *I* is a fact. Second, we must remember this fact. Third, we must analyze this fact. Here are two Comforters. The Lord says, "I will ask the Father, and He [the Father] will give you another Comforter." The word *another* in the expression *another Comforter* means this is the second one. "And He [the Father] will give you another Comforter." This means that the Father will give a second Comforter. If there is a second Comforter, there must be a first Comforter.

The first thing we can ascertain is that the Lord is speaking of two Comforters. The Lord said that the disciples already had one Comforter, but that He was going to give them another. What kind of Comforter is the second? "That He may be with you forever." Who is the *He*? The Lord Jesus said, "The world...does not...know Him; but you know Him." Why? "Because He abides with you." He was with them all the time. The world cannot receive Him and has not even seen Him. What about them? The disciples had seen Him; they knew Him. They knew Him because He was abiding with them all the time.

The Lord said, "Because He abides with you and shall be in you." After this point the pronoun *He* is no longer used. In the next sentence the Lord said, "I will not leave you as orphans; I am coming to you." In studying this, we find that *He* is *I,* and *I* is *He.* In other words, while the Lord Jesus was living on earth, He was the Comforter. The Holy Spirit was in the Lord, and the Lord was the Comforter. When the Lord was on earth, the Holy Spirit was in Him; He and the Holy Spirit were one. This is why He said that the disciples beheld Him and knew Him and that He was with them.

But then what happened? The Lord went on to tell them that another Comforter would come. Following His death and resurrection, the Lord said that He would come back to them and that God would give them the Holy Spirit. But how was this to be accomplished? The Lord Himself would come to them again in the Holy Spirit. He did not leave them orphans. After a little while they would see Him no longer, but then they would see Him again, and He would abide in them. Verse 17 says, "He...in you." Then verse 20 says, "I in you." Thus, the *I* in the second section is the *He* in the first section. Once we see the change in pronouns, we see the difference in the two Comforters. The first section refers to the Holy Spirit in Christ. The second section refers to Christ in the Holy Spirit. *He* refers to the Holy Spirit in Christ. *I* refers to Christ in the Holy Spirit. Who is the Holy Spirit? The Holy Spirit is the Lord Jesus in another form. The Son is the Father in another form. In the same way, the Holy Spirit is the Son in another form. There is only a change in form.

From this example we see that the first basic principle in reading the Bible is to discover the facts. If we cannot discover any facts, we cannot expect to receive any light from God. It is not a question of how many times we have read the Bible, but a question of the facts we have discovered through our many times of reading.

Paul was a person who knew how to discover facts. Consider what he said in Galatians 3. He saw from Genesis that God would bless the nations through the seed of Abraham. God used the word *seed* in its singular form, not in its plural form. This refers to Christ. First, Paul discovered this fact. He saw that the nations would be blessed through the seed of Abraham, and he saw that this was a unique seed. From this he realized that this seed referred to Christ. If it had been plural, it would have referred to the many children of Abraham, that is, the Jews, and the meaning would be completely different. Paul read the Scripture thoroughly and discovered the facts.

In the Bible there are many facts. Whether or not a person is rich in God's Word depends on how many facts he has discovered. The more facts he discovers, the richer he becomes. If he cannot discover any facts and if he reads through the Bible in a hasty and mindless way, he will not understand much.

In reading the Bible, we must learn to discover the facts. After this we should memorize, analyze, and compare these facts. Finally, we should kneel down before God and ask for light.

III. DIFFERENT WAYS TO READ THE BIBLE

We should read our Bible during two different periods of time. We should have two copies of the Bible for these two occasions. One period can be in the morning and the other in the afternoon. Or we can do both early in the morning by reading one way during the first half of our time and another way during the second half of our time. These two periods of time must be separate. In the morning period or the first half of the early morning reading, we should meditate, praise, and pray as we read the Word, mixing our reading with meditation, praise, and prayer. This period of reading is for receiving spiritual food and for strengthening our spirit. Do not read too much during this time; three or four verses is sufficient. The afternoon time, or the second half of the early morning reading, should be longer. During this time, we should read for the purpose of learning more about God's Word.

If possible, we should have two Bibles. The Bible used in the first period should not have any marks or notes written in it (except dates, which we will mention later). The Bible used in the second period can contain whatever we have been touched with, either by jotting down notes or by circling or underlining words or passages. The Bible used in the first period can contain dates—dates on which we came across a special verse, made a deal with the Lord, or had a special experience. We should write down the date next to such a verse, indicating that we met God through this verse on that date. Do not write down anything other than dates. The Bible used in the second period is for understanding, and we should write down all the spiritual facts we discover and the light we have received. Now let us discuss the way to read the Bible during these two periods of time.

A. Meditating on the Word
during the First Period of Time

Concerning meditating on the Word, I think the best thing is for me to quote George Müller. He said:

It has recently pleased the Lord to teach me a truth, irrespective of human instrumentality, as far as I know, the benefit of which I have not lost, though now, while preparing the fifth edition for the press, more than fourteen years have since passed away. The point is this: I saw more clearly than ever that the first great and primary business to which I ought to attend every day was, to have my soul happy in the Lord. The first thing to be concerned about was not how much I might serve the Lord, how I might glorify the Lord; but how I might get my soul into a happy state, and how my inner man might be nourished. For I might seek to set the truth before the unconverted, I might seek to benefit believers, I might seek to relieve the distressed, I might in other ways seek to behave myself as it becomes a child of God in this world; and yet, not being happy in the Lord, and not being nourished and strengthened in my inner man day by day, all this might not be attended to in a right spirit. Before this time my practice had been, at least for ten years previously, as an habitual thing to give myself to in prayer, after having dressed myself in the morning. *Now,* I saw that the most important thing I had to do was to give myself to the reading of the word of God, and to meditation on it, that thus my heart might be comforted, encouraged, warned, reproved, instructed; and that thus, by means of the word of God, whilst meditating on it, my heart might be brought into experimental communion with the Lord.

I began therefore to meditate on the New Testament from the beginning, early in the morning. The first thing I did, after having asked in a few words the Lord's blessing upon his precious word, was, to begin to meditate on the word of God, searching as it were into every verse, to get blessing out of it; not for the sake of the public ministry of the word, not for the sake of preaching on what I had meditated upon, but for the sake of obtaining food for my own soul. The result I have found to be almost invariably this, that after a very few minutes my soul has been led to confession, or to thanksgiving, or to intercession, or to supplication; so that, though I did not, as it were, give myself to *prayer,* but to *meditation,* yet it turned almost immediately more or less into prayer. When thus I have been for a while making confession, or intercession, or supplication, or have given thanks, I go on to the next words or verse, turning all, as I go on, into prayer for myself or others, as the word may lead to it, but still continually keeping before me that food for my own soul is the object of my meditation. The result of this is, that there is always a good deal of confession, thanksgiving, supplication, or intercession mingled with my meditation, and that my inner man almost invariably is even sensibly nourished and strengthened, and that by breakfast time, with rare exceptions, I am in a peaceful if not happy state of heart. Thus also the Lord is pleased to communicate unto me that which, either very soon after or at a later time, I have found to become food for other believers, though it was not for the sake of the public ministry of the word that I gave myself to meditation, but for the profit of my own inner man....

And yet now, since God has taught me this point, it is as plain to me as anything, that the first thing the child of God has to do morning by morning is, to *obtain food for his inner man.* As the outward man is not fit for work for any length of time except we take food, and as this is one of the first things we do in the morning, so it should be with the inner man. We should take food for that, as every one must allow. Now what is the food for the inner man? Not *prayer,* but *the word of God;* and here again, not the simple reading of the word of God, so that it only passes through our minds, just as water runs through a pipe, but considering what we read, pondering over it, and applying it to our hearts. When we pray, we speak to God. Now, prayer, in order to be continued for any length of time in any other than a formal manner, requires, generally speaking, a measure of strength or godly desire, and the season, therefore, when this exercise of the soul can be most effectually performed is after the inner man has been nourished by meditation on the word of God, where we find our Father speaking to us, to encourage us, to comfort us, to instruct us, to humble us, to reprove us. We may therefore profitably meditate, with God's blessing, though we are ever so weak spiritually; nay, the weaker we are, the more we need meditation for the strengthening of our inner man. There is thus far less to be feared from wandering of mind than if we give ourselves to prayer without having had previously time for meditation. I dwell so particularly on this point because of the immense spiritual profit and refreshment I am conscious of having derived from it myself, and I affectionately and solemnly beseech all my fellow-believers to ponder this matter. By the blessing of God I ascribe to this mode the help and strength which I had had from God to pass in peace through deeper trials, in various ways, than I had ever had before; and after having now above fourteen years tried this way, I can most fully, in the fear of God, commend it....

How different, when the soul is refreshed and made happy early in the morning, from what it is when, without spiritual preparation, the service, the trials, and the temptations of the day come upon one!—George Müller, *Autobiography of George Müller, the Life of Trust,* 1861, reprinted 1981, pp. 206-10.

B. General Reading
during the Second Period of Time

A new believer who recently has received the Lord should not engage himself in intense research of the Bible for at least six months because he is not familiar with the Bible as a whole yet. He should rather spend a few months to read through the whole Bible and familiarize himself with it in a general way. After this he can begin serious study of the Bible.

In familiarizing himself with the Bible, he should read the whole book chapter by chapter, consecutively over and over again. The best way is to decide the number of chapters in the Old and the New Testament one wants to read each day. The reading should neither be too fast nor too slow. It should be regular, continuous, and general in nature. George Müller read the Old and New Testament a hundred times during his lifetime. Those who have just received the Lord should learn to read the Bible and remember the number of times they have read through it. It is good to write a letter to notify a more elderly brother the first time you have finished reading through the New Testament. It is also good to leave a blank page in your Bible to record the number of times you have read through it. You should write the date and the place you finished reading it the first time, the second time, and so on. Each time you finish reading it, you should mark down the occasion. Identify clearly whether it is the Old Testament or the New Testament you have read through. I hope that you, like Mr. Müller, can read through the Bible a hundred times during your lifetime. If a person wants to read through the Bible a hundred times, assuming that he lives for fifty years as a Christian, he will have to go through the whole Bible at least twice a year. You can see why you need to spend much time to read the Bible.

The principle of reading the Bible is to go through it chapter by chapter, over and over again. Those who are more advanced in the Lord should pay attention to the way the newly saved ones read their Bibles. Sometimes it does good to examine the dates recorded in their Bibles, to check how many chapters they read every day, and to find out where they are each week. We should all pay attention to this work and should not slacken. We should remind those who are progressing too slowly, "Half a year has past. How come you have not finished reading the New Testament once yet?"

If a person reads his Bible according to the above way, after some time his knowledge of the Bible will increase. If possible, one should try to memorize one or two verses each day. In the beginning, a person may have to force himself a little to do this. It may come as quite a dull chore. But after some time he will reap the benefit of it.

C. Intense Study
during a Specifically Apportioned Time

The first kind of daily Bible reading—praying and meditating over the Word—is a continuous lifelong practice. The second kind of reading—general reading, involving some kind of Bible study—can begin after at least six months are spent gaining some knowledge of the Bible.

Every Christian should have a definite plan of studying the Bible. If you can set aside half an hour a day, develop a plan to study the Bible for half an hour a day. If you can afford an hour each day, develop a plan that includes an hour of study. Whatever time you can afford, make a plan that will fit your schedule. The worst way to read is by "inspiration," that is, casual, unplanned reading that begins at whatever page one feels, at times reading voraciously for ten days and at other times not reading anything for ten days. This is the wrong way. We should not adopt this "inspirational" method.

Everyone should have a definite plan of reading. In reading the Bible, we need to be restricted and disciplined.

However, do not set too high a standard or too long a time for yourself. If you set too long a time, it will be hard to maintain the schedule. This is worse than having no plan at all. Once you decide to do something, stick to it for five years, ten years, or fifteen years. Do not stop after two, three, five, or six months. This is why you should consider carefully before the Lord the amount of time you should set aside for your study. One hour each day should be quite sufficient. Half an hour may be too short; one may not get much done in half an hour. Of course, if time does not allow you to have an hour, half an hour is still good. One hour, however, is the optimum period of time. If one can afford two hours, it is good. Normally, there is no need to spend more than two hours. We have not seen a brother or sister who studies for three hours a day who can maintain this schedule for long.

There are twenty-eight different ways to study the Bible, which are covered in the book *The Ways to Study the Bible*. Of the twenty-eight ways, the study of the progression of truth throughout the Bible is the most difficult. For many people, this method should not be attempted until a much later time. The method of word study is a much easier approach. One can also study metals, minerals, numbers, names of persons, geography, etc. These can be supplementary studies; we do not have to devote all our time to these special ways. There are also the chronologies in the Bible. If we have the time, we can take a look at them. Besides these, there are other ways to study the Bible, like studying prophecies, types, parables, miracles, the Lord's teaching on earth, or doing a book-by-book study, etc. We should go through all these methods one by one.

Let us assume for now that a person has one hour a day to study the Bible. He can allocate his time in the following way:

1. First Twenty Minutes—Studying by Subjects

The experience of some people suggests that an hour of study can be divided into four sessions. The first session of twenty minutes is for studying specific subjects like prophecies, types, parables, dispensations, the Lord's teachings on earth, or a specific book. One can read all the related passages and find the verses that deal with the subject chosen. If one is trying to study one book at a time, he should select the book he wants to study. He may choose Romans or the Gospel of John. After he finishes one book, he should go on to the next. He should study the whole book and find out the content of each book. If you decide to dedicate twenty minutes of your time each day to this kind of study, do not prolong or shorten it. We must learn to restrict ourselves and never be a careless or loose person.

2. The Second Twenty Minutes—Word Study

The second twenty minutes can be used for word study. There are many special terms like *reconciliation, blood, faith, joy, peace, hope, love, obedience, righteousness, redemption, mercy, etc.,* which are scattered throughout the Bible, and they all are very meaningful. If they are grouped and compiled together, we can get a better grasp of their meaning. For example, we may study the word *blood.* First, we should jot down all the chapters and verses that mention the blood. Then we should analyze the meaning of each occurrence. What has the blood done for us before God? What type of persons does the blood deal with? What and how much has the blood accomplished for us? In the Old and New Testament, we can find many verses which speak of the blood. We can analyze them all. This cannot be accomplished in one sitting. One cannot hope to see much result on the first day. If he has access to a concordance, he can save much labor.

3. The Third Ten Minutes—Gathering Information

One can choose specific topics and spend the next ten minutes solely gathering information concerning them. There are many topics in the Bible, such as creation, man, sin, salvation, repentance, the Holy Spirit, regeneration, sanctification, justification, forgiveness, freedom, the Body of Christ, the Lord's coming, judgment, the kingdom, eternity, etc. You can choose certain topics and then gather information about them from the Bible. The most one can handle at one time is five topics; if there are more than five topics, there will be too many clues, and it will be difficult to handle them all at once. Do not gather material for one topic alone; this is too time consuming. One may find material for more than one topic in a chapter. For example, you may be studying about the Holy Spirit. But the particular chapter you are on may not have anything on the Holy Spirit. But you can definitely find other topics in the same chapter. It is not a bad idea to gather information on two, three, four, or five topics at the same time. But do not take more than five at one time.

Each topic may require some time to complete its study. Every day you have to add more material to your study. Write down all the materials (verses) you have gathered, and from these write down the main words and meanings of each passage. It is useless to merely jot down the verses. You must know what the verses are saying. Suppose you are studying the Holy Spirit in Ephesians. In writing down "sealed with the Holy Spirit" in 1:13, you should also write down the meaning of the word *seal*. First, write down the verse, then the related terms, and finally the meaning of the verse. You should gather all the information this way. One day when you need to deal with such a topic, these materials will be on hand for you to apply.

4. The Fourth Ten Minutes—Paraphrasing

The final ten minutes can be used to paraphrase the Bible. This exercise is very useful. Paraphrasing the Bible gives fresh insight into a passage. By paraphrasing the Bible with simple words, we express a passage in a way that others can understand at a glance.

For example, you may be doing a chapter-by-chapter study of the book of Romans. If a teen-ager comes and says, "I have read Paul's word in Romans, but I cannot understand it," you will have to think of some ways to explain this book to him using your own words. A paraphrase is not a commentary; you are merely using your own words to convey what Paul said so that those who do not understand it can understand.

In order to do this, you have to learn to paraphrase the Bible
with your own words. Take the book of Romans and try to
paraphrase it with your own words. Paul wrote the Epistles
in his words. Now you should try to write the same thing
in your own words. Try your best to do this. Do it properly
and intelligently so that you can understand it and so that
other brothers and sisters who read it can understand it as
well.

Such paraphrasing will show how well we know the Scriptures. Using our own words to reiterate the apostles' thought is
a good way to prepare us for biblical exposition. Paraphrasing
is the first step; exposition is the second step. First we should
learn to paraphrase the text of the Bible with our own words.
Our training before God must be in the proper order. Do not
try to expound the Bible before learning to paraphrase it; this
is too hasty. Learn to paraphrase the Bible first and then
learn to expound it. If we cannot paraphrase the Bible well, it
is impossible for us to expound it well. We must paraphrase
first and then expound. We must all learn this basic lesson.
First, paraphrase Paul's Epistles, then paraphrase the remain-
der of the New Testament.

In paraphrasing the Bible, try to avoid using the words of
the Bible. Use your own words instead. The main lesson to
learn here is to express the meaning of a passage with words
that are within your grasp. After you have tried one book, you
will know how precious the experience is and how profitable
the exercise is. A careless and sloppy person cannot paraphrase
the Bible. You must pray much before the Lord and read the
Bible properly before you can paraphrase it correctly. After
you finish a book, go back and revise your work once or twice,
modifying it with appropriate words and polishing your
sentences. This will give you a better impression of the book,
and you will come to know what the apostles were talking
about. You need to paraphrase a passage before you can have
a deep impression of it.

In order to paraphrase the Bible, one must first study it
thoroughly. He must understand what a passage says and
what is implied in the passage. He can then incorporate all
his knowledge into his paraphrase. This requires a thorough

understanding of a verse. A person can only paraphrase the Bible when he has a clear grasp of what it says. Through practicing a little every day, and through careful reading and meticulous writing, one will eventually be able to paraphrase one of Paul's Epistles. He will then be able to understand Paul's word and will be able to use other words to convey the same meaning.

We have mentioned four things already. First, study by topic; second, do a word study; third, gather information; and fourth, paraphrase. We should go through all twenty-eight methods one by one. A definite schedule of Bible study is an exercise for us. We must gird up our loins, be restricted and regulated before the Lord, and not be loose. If we have made up our mind to study for an hour, keep this hour. We should not shorten or lengthen the time, unless we are sick or on vacation. Other than such exceptions, we should always keep our schedule. If we persist in this exercise daily, we will soon reap the harvest.